314

Collaborative Class Books
From A to Z

by Ada Goren

NEW YORK ● TORONTO ● LONDON ● AUCKLAND ● SYDNEY
MEXICO CITY ● NEW DELHI ● HONG KONG ● BUENOS AIRES

Teaching *Resources*

To my coworkers at

Messiah Moravian Preschool

Edited by Immacula A. Rhodes
Cover design by Scott Davis
Interior design by Kathy Massaro
Interior photos by Scott Davis

ISBN 978-0-545-49624-7

1 2 3 4 5 6 7 8 9 10   40   21 20 19 18 17 16 15 14

Contents

❄ ❋ ❄   **Collaborative Class Books**   ❄ ❋ ❄

Introduction

There's no question that learning the alphabet and the sounds associated with each letter are the very cornerstones of reading and writing proficiency. The ideas presented in *Collaborative Class Books From A to Z* make learning letters and their sounds a fun—and personalized—experience for children.

All teachers understand that reading aloud is an invaluable component of reading instruction. And when children attempt to "read" books independently, they are practicing important skills in recognizing words and comprehending text. That's where collaborative class books have a distinct advantage! By featuring predictable text paired with children's own ideas, work, photos, and names, the student-made books in this resource have personal appeal to students. Besides promoting literacy learning, these collaborative books also encourage cooperation. Each child contributes to the project, and the class as a whole produces a wonderful finished book!

As you introduce or focus on each letter of the alphabet, invite children to create a class book for that letter. You can present the books in order, use them to reinforce particular letter skills, or connect them to a particular thematic unit. For example, you might create "Lovely Ladybugs" when your class is studying insects or "Our Rectangle Robots" when children are learning about shapes. No matter when your class creates these books, they'll provide lots of learning and sharing opportunities for children. And no doubt, they'll ask to read—and have these books read to them—again and again. You'll soon discover that these will be the first books children choose from the classroom library to enjoy.

What's Inside

Each letter unit includes easy-to-follow directions for making the collaborative class book for that letter. The books include a variety of formats and are constructed from easily available materials. On each set of instructional pages, you'll find:

❋ an activity to introduce the feature letter to children and ease them into the topic for the class book

❋ any preparation you need to complete before starting the class project

❋ a list of materials needed to create the book pages and cover and for binding the book

❋ literacy skills, including sight words, addressed by the book

❋ directions for making the cover and pages

To help meet the learning needs of your students, check page 7 to see how activities in this book link to the Common Core State Standards for Reading (Foundational Skills).

- one or more tips to simplify preparing the materials, constructing the book, or enhancing the pages

- directions for assembling the book

- a follow-up activity to extend learning

On pages 60–80 of this resource, you'll find reproducible pages that make assembling these class books a snap! In addition to patterns, reproducible text boxes are provided for most of the books to help save time in writing text on the pages and to allow children to personalize their pages. Children can fill in the blanks on the text boxes themselves to complete the text, or dictate responses for you or a class volunteer to write.

Binding the Books

With the exception of the accordion-folded class books, you'll find that all the assembly directions call for you to punch holes and use rings to bind the class books. You can use either metal (similar to key rings) or plastic rings for binding. However, you have a number of other binding options you might want to use to make each class book a bit more fun and unique. Following are a few ideas:

- **Use colorful ribbon or yarn.** After punching holes, thread a length of decorative ribbon or colorful yarn through the holes in the stacked pages. Either tie a knot or small bow, then trim away any excess ribbon or yarn.

- **Use a rubber band and large paper clip.** Punch two holes a little farther apart than the length of a jumbo paper clip. Thread the two ends of a rubber band through the holes and then attach each end to a jumbo paper clip to hold the rubber band taut. You can use colorful rubber bands and clips, or even use a colorful ponytail holder in place of the rubber band. (If you plan to bind a paper-plate book with this method, use a small paper clip.)

- **Use staples.** In a hurry? If so, or if the class book is a thin one, you can simply staple the pages together. If available, colored staples add a nice touch.

- **Use a book-binding machine.** If you have access to a comb binder, this machine can make binding your books simple. The binding combs come in a variety of sizes, to accommodate various thicknesses.

Important Tips

- Have a black marker, scissors, and glue on hand when making the class books. You'll need one or more of these materials for all books.

- Children can cut out the text boxes and patterns for their book pages, or you can precut these for children in advance.

- If the text on a book page does not include the student's name, write his or her name somewhere on the front or back of the page.

- In advance, make a student page for each book to become familiar with the directions and materials. You can then display the page for children to use as a model when making their own pages.

- Apply sturdy hole reinforcers to the holes in each book cover and page to help prevent the holes from being torn or worn out from use.

To Laminate or Not to Laminate

Laminating the pages of much-loved and well-used books can prolong their life and help them stand up better to repeated handling by little hands. But not all of the books in this resource lend themselves to lamination. While there are no suggestions provided for laminating the book covers or pages, here are a few factors to consider when deciding whether or not to laminate them:

❋ Do you have easy access to a laminator?

❋ Is the use of the laminator cost-free or inexpensive?

❋ Do you have time to laminate the book covers and/or pages? (Perhaps a parent volunteer might be willing to take on this task.)

When considering the option of laminating, keep in mind that any covers or pages created with craft materials that add texture will not laminate well-running these through a laminator can damage both the pages and the machine. And if you plan to laminate pages that have flaps, you will need to re-cut the flaps. (The area under the flap will not be laminated.)

Using the Collaborative Class Books

The most obvious way to use your completed class books is to read them with your class! Children will enjoy hearing their books read aloud over and over again. But there are many other ways you can use the books. Following are a few ideas:

❋ Feature one of the books as the "Book of the Week." Place the selected book on a stand or display it in a special place.

❋ When you need a five-minute filler, bring out one of your class books for a special reading time.

❋ Revisit previously made class books when they fit a theme or topic currently being studied. For example if the class made "Meet Our Monsters!" near the start of your school year, you might bring it out to reread for Halloween.

❋ Invite children who are proficient at reading a particular class book to read it aloud to another teacher, a volunteer, or the school principal.

❋ Allow children to "check out" the class books overnight to share with their families. Parents will love to see the work and photos of their own child, as well as those of their child's classmates.

❋ Put the class books on display at an Open House or Parents' Night. Invite children to read their pages to their families.

❋ At the end of the school year, hold a lottery. Draw children's names from a bag and allow those children to choose a class book to take home as a keepsake.

Create a special storage area in your reading center or class library just for your class-made books. Make sure children have easy access to the area so they can retrieve the books when ready to read them.

Connections to the Common Core State Standards

The Common Core State Standards Initiative (CCSSI) has outlined learning expectations in English Language Arts for students at different grade levels. The activities in this book align with the following Foundational Skills for Reading for students in grades K–1. For more information, visit the CCSSI website at www.corestandards.org.

Print Concepts

- RF.K.1, RF.1.1. Demonstrate understanding of the organization and basic features of print.
- RF.K.1a. Follow words from left to right, top to bottom, and page by page.
- RF.K.1b. Recognize that spoken words are represented in written language by specific sequences of letters.
- RF.K.1d. Recognize and name all upper- and lowercase letters of the alphabet.

Phonological Awareness

- RF.K.2, RF.1.2. Demonstrate understanding of spoken words, syllables, and sounds (phonemes).
- RF.K.2b. Count, pronounce, blend, and segment syllables in spoken words.
- RF.K.2c. Blend and segment onsets and rimes of single-syllable spoken words.
- RF.1.2b. Orally produce single-syllable words by blending sounds (phonemes), including consonant blends.

Phonics and Word Recognition

- RF.K.3, RF.1.3. Know and apply grade-level phonics and word analysis skills in decoding words.
- RF.K.3a. Demonstrate basic knowledge of one-to-one letter-sound correspondences by producing the primary sound or many of the most frequent sounds for each consonant.
- RF.K.3b. Associate the long and short sounds with the common spellings (graphemes) for the five major vowels.
- RF.K.3c. Read common high-frequency words by sight (e.g., *the, of, to, you, she, my, is, are, do, does*).
- RF.1.3g. Recognize and read grade-appropriate irregularly spelled words.

Fluency

- RF.K.4. Read emergent-reader texts with purpose and understanding.
- RF.1.4. Read with sufficient accuracy and fluency to support comprehension.
- RF.1.4a. Read grade-level text with purpose and understanding.
- RF.1.4c. Use context to confirm or self-correct word recognition and understanding, rereading as necessary.

The Ants Went Marching By...

Skills

* Concepts of print
* Long and short sounds of *A*
* Sight words: *an*, *and*, *by*, *the*, *went*

✂ Materials

* 9- by 12-inch sheet of white construction paper (for the cover)
* 9- by 12-inch red construction paper, one per child, plus one for the title page
* $3\frac{1}{2}$- by 12-inch white construction paper, one per child, plus one for the title page
* pictures of items that begin with *A*
* green crayons
* black tempera paint
* black marker
* clear tape

Introduce the Letter

❋ ❋ ❋

Invite children to join in a rousing rendition of the traditional song "The Ants Go Marching." After singing, point out that *ants* begins with the letter *A*. Show children a letter card labeled with an uppercase and lowercase *Aa*. Then explain that the class will create a book about things beginning with *A* that those ants just might have encountered as they marched along!

Get Ready

Gather and cut out a supply of pictures that show items beginning with the letter *A* (both long and short sounds of the letter). Use magazines, as well as images printed from the Internet and your clip-art collection. Provide at least one picture for each child.

Make the Cover and Title Page
(for teacher)

1. To make the cover, label the white construction paper with the title "The Ants Went Marching By..." and add an author line.

2. Add a checkered background—to resemble a picnic cloth—and a few fingerprint ants. (See step 4 in Make the Pages.)

3. For the title page, follow steps 1, 2, and 4 in Make the Pages. Write the title text above the grass line, this time using a capital letter only for the first word.

4. Glue the cover and title page together back-to-back.

Make the Pages *(for students)*

1. Glue the white paper strip to the bottom of the red paper.

2. Use a green crayon to draw grass on the white strip.

3. Choose a letter *A* picture. Glue it to the center of the page along the top of the grass line.

4. Use the black paint to make a few fingerprint ants in the grass. (Check that each ant has these three body parts: a head, a thorax, and abdomen.) When the paint dries, add six legs and two antennae with the black marker.

5. Have your teacher add text to your page, including the *A* word that names your picture (as shown).

For added texture, glue short strips of green paper to the grassy section.

The ants went marching by...

an alligator,

an apple,

Assemble the Book

1. Place the cover facedown.

2. Use clear tape to connect the student pages to each other side by side. Tape the first student page to the title page, as shown.

3. Fold the pages back and forth, accordion-style, so that the cover is faceup on the top of the stack.

More Letter Learning

Explore even more words that begin with *A* by reading aloud *Berenstains' A Book* by Stan and Jan Berenstain (Random House Books for Young Readers, 1997). Afterward, have children search the room to find objects and words that begin with *A*.

Our Boo-Boo Book

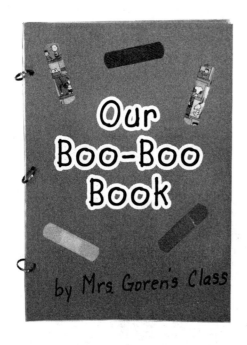

Introduce the Letter

❄ ❄ ❄

Read aloud the rhyming and interactive *The Boo-Boo Book* by Joy Masoff (Lark Books, 2006). Point out that *boo-boo* begins with the letter *B*. Show children a letter card labeled with an uppercase and lowercase *Bb*. Next, invite them to regale you with tales of their own boo-boos. Finally, ask children to document the healing powers of a simple bandaid as they create pages for this engaging class book.

Skills

❄ Concepts of print
❄ Beginning sound of *B*
❄ Sight words: *a, better, has, he, her, his, it, make, on, put, she, to*

✂ Materials

- 10- by 14-inch construction paper, one per child, plus one for the cover
- class supply of bandaids (plus a few extra for the cover)
- close-up photo of each child
- text box (page 60), one per child
- hole punch
- three metal or plastic rings (for binding)

Get Ready

Take a close-up digital photo of each child's face. Print each photo (in color or in black and white) onto copy paper, filling up the entire page with the image. Also copy and cut out a class supply of the text box on page 60, checking that you have one text box with the appropriate pronoun for each boy and girl in your class.

Make the Cover *(for teacher)*

1. Label a 10- by 14-inch sheet of construction paper with the title "Our Boo-Boo Book" and add an author line.

2. Affix a few colorful or printed bandaids to the page around the title.

Make the Pages *(for students)*

1. Glue your photo near the top of a sheet of construction paper.

2. Peel the backing off a bandaid. Stick it to one part of your face on the photo (such as on your nose, cheek, or forehead) to mark an imaginary "boo-boo."

3. Have your teacher complete a text box with your name and location of your boo-boo.

4. Glue the text box below your photo.

Assemble the Book

1. Stack the student pages in any order desired. Place the cover on top.

2. Punch three holes along the left edge of each page, aligning the holes in all of the pages.

3. Use three rings to bind the pages together.

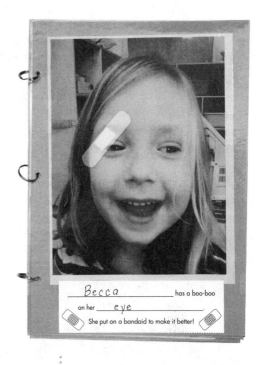

Becca has a boo-boo
on her eye
She put on a bandaid to make it better!

Tip

For added fun, provide bandaids in different sizes, shapes, and colors, including some printed with designs or characters.

More Letter Learning

Give each child a copy of a large letter *B*, printed in a simple black line. Provide a supply of inexpensive bandaids. Then ask children to peel and stick bandaids along the lines to form a bandaid *B*.

Cc

Colorful, Colossal Cupcakes

Colorful,
Colossal
Cupcakes

by
Mrs. Kraft's
Class

Skills

❈ Concepts of print
❈ Hard sound of C
❈ Sight words: *has*, *is*, *the*, *this*
❈ Color words

✂ Materials

- tagboard templates of cupcake top and bottom (pages 61–62)
- 9- by 12-inch and 12- by 18-inch construction paper in various colors (one of each size per child and for the cover)
- craft items, such as dot markers and paper-punch, craft-foam, and confetti shapes (for cupcake decorations)
- text box (page 62), one per child
- hole punch
- two metal or plastic rings (for binding)

Introduce the Letter

❈ ❈ ❈

Ask children, "What is your favorite kind of cupcake?" Invite them to discuss their favorite flavors, colors, or decorations. Then tell children that they will make gigantic cupcake pages of their own design to use in a class book. Before beginning this sweet, oversized project, point out that *cupcakes* begins with the letter *C*. Show children a letter card labeled with an uppercase and lowercase *Cc*. Also, introduce the words *colossal* and *confetti* and the beginning sound in these words.

Get Ready

Copy the top and bottom cupcake templates (pages 61–62) onto several sheets of tagboard and cut out.

Make the Cover *(for teacher)*

1. Follow steps 1 through 4 in Make the Pages to make a cupcake-shaped cover.

2. Label the top of the cupcake with "Colorful, Colossal Cupcakes." Add "confetti" craft items around the title, if desired.

3. Add an author line to the bottom part of the cupcake.

Make the Pages *(for students)*

1. Take one sheet of each construction paper size, choosing the desired colors for your cupcake top and bottom. Fold each sheet in half horizontally.

2. Place the template for the cupcake top along the fold of the large sheet of paper and trace around it. Cut out the shape through all layers and unfold.

3. Repeat step 2, using the template for the cupcake bottom and the small sheet of paper.

4. Glue your cupcake top to the bottom.

5. Add "confetti" to your cupcake top, using the craft items in the color of your choice.

6. Have your teacher complete a text box with your name and dictated description of your cupcake.

7. Glue the text box to the bottom section of your cupcake.

Assemble the Book

1. Stack the student pages in any order desired. Place the cover on top.

2. Punch two holes at the top of each page, aligning the holes in all of the pages.

3. Use two rings to bind the pages together.

Ellie's
colossal cupcake is
the color yellow.
This cupcake has
orange confetti.

Use patterned scrapbook paper for the cupcake bottoms to make them resemble decorative cupcake liners.

More Letter Learning

Enjoy an entertaining story about cupcakes by reading aloud *If You Give a Cat a Cupcake* by Laura Joffe Numeroff (HarperCollins, 2008). Afterward, you might make actual cupcakes with the class. As you prepare the cupcakes, emphasize the beginning sound of any cooking tools, directions, or ingredients that begin with *C*, such as *cup, cool, careful, clean,* and *confetti.*

Note: Be sure to check in advance for any food allergies.

Ding-Dong! Who's at the Door?

Introduce children to the letter *D* with a special delivery. Put a few small items that begin with *D* (e.g., a doll, toy dinosaur, diamond cutout, and dime) into a small box. Seal the box and address it to your class. Arrange for a colleague to put the box outside your door and loudly say, "Ding-dong!" during your group time. Retrieve and open the box, then remove and name each item inside it. Ask children to tell what all the items have in common (*they begin with* D). Then display a letter card labeled with an uppercase and lowercase *Dd*. Finally, invite children to make pages for this book about some special letter *D* deliveries!

Skills

✳ Concepts of print
✳ Beginning sound of *D*
✳ Sight words: *a, at, the, with*

 ## Materials

● 9- by 12-inch construction paper, one sheet per child, plus one for the cover
● 4- by 5-inch photo of each student
● introduction text box (page 63), one per child
● door text box (page 63), one per child, plus one for the cover
● crayons
● hole punch
● two metal or plastic rings (for binding)

Get Ready

Take a digital photo of each child standing in your classroom doorway and holding an item that begins with *D*. Print the photos and trim each to about 4 by 5 inches.

Make the Cover *(for teacher)*

1. Label a sheet of construction paper with the title "Ding-Dong! Who's at the Door?"

2. Color and cut out the door part of the door text box (page 63).

3. Glue the door to the bottom of the page, gluing only the left side to create a flap.

4. Write the author line on the page under the flap.

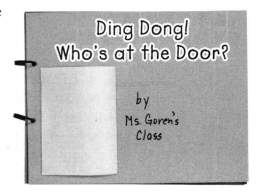

Collaborative Class Books From A to Z © 2014 by Ada Goren, Scholastic Teaching Resources

Make the Pages *(for students)*

1. Glue the introduction text box to the top of your page, as shown.

2. Glue your photo near the bottom of the page at the middle.

3. Color the door on the door text box. Fold the cutout in half and glue the two sides together back-to-back.

4. Ask your teacher to fill in the text box on the back of the door with your name and the item you are holding in the picture. (This will be a *D* word.)

5. Glue the door over your picture, gluing only along the left side to make a flap.

Assemble the Book

1. Stack the student pages in any order desired. Place the cover on top.

2. Punch two holes along the left edge of each page, aligning the holes in all of the pages.

3. Use two rings to bind the pages together.

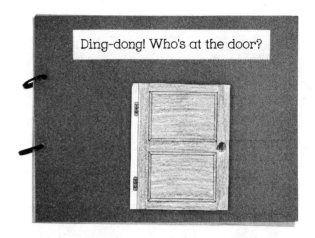

More Letter Learning

Use this super-simple craft to help children remember the connection between the letter *D* and the word *door*. Cut out a large letter *D* for each child from construction paper, but do not cut out the center. Draw a solid straight line and a dotted curved line on each cutout, as shown. Then help children cut along the dotted line and fold the flap back on the solid line to create a door in their letter. If desired, they can draw a large dot for a doorknob on their door.

Tip

Check that children have centered the door over their photo before they glue it in place. When the door is closed, the picture will not show, but it will appear when the door is opened.

Extraordinary Eggs

Introduce the Letter

❈ ❈ ❈

Show children a white paper cutout of an egg. Point out that *egg* begins with the letter *E*. Then display a letter card labeled with an uppercase and lowercase *Ee*. Next, ask children to describe the egg. Is it small, or is it *enormous*? How might they make an ordinary paper egg look different, more interesting, *extraordinary*? After sharing, invite children to convert large, plain paper eggs into extraordinary eggs for your class book.

Skills

❈ Concepts of print
❈ Short and long sounds of *E*
❈ Sight words: *because, is, it*

✂ Materials

- 12- by 18-inch black construction paper, one per child, plus one for the cover
- large white construction-paper eggs, one per child, plus one for the cover
- craft materials, such as glitter glue, craft-foam and paper-punch shapes, and confetti (to decorate eggs)
- white copy paper (for the cover title)
- text box (page 64), one per child
- hole punch
- two metal or plastic rings (for binding)

Get Ready

Cut a supply of large eggs from 9- by 12-inch sheets of white construction paper.

Make the Cover (for teacher)

1. Follow steps 1 and 2 in Make the Pages to decorate the cover.

2. Write the title "Extraordinary Eggs" and an author line on the white paper. Cut an irregular-shaped outline around the text, then glue below the egg.

Make the Pages *(for students)*

1. Choose a craft material. Use it to decorate your egg.

2. Glue your egg to the top part of a sheet of black construction paper.

3. Ask your teacher to fill in your text box with your name and dictated description of your egg.

4. Glue the text box below your egg.

Assemble the Book

1. Stack the student pages in any order desired. Place the cover on top.

2. Punch two holes along the top edge of each page, aligning the holes in all of the pages.

3. Use two rings to bind the pages together.

Talia's
enormous egg is extraordinary
because it *has lots of colors and shapes*

Check that the glue on children's pages is thoroughly dry before assembling the book.

More Letter Learning

To reinforce the letter-sound association of *E*, give children another egg shape, this time cut from white copy paper. Provide markers or crayons and have children write *E* repeatedly on their egg, covering the entire shape with the letter in a variety of colors.

Funny Faces

Introduce the Letter

❉ ❉ ❉

Show children a letter card labeled with an uppercase and lowercase *Ff*. Name some words that begin with *F*, including the word *face*. Then have children identify the different parts of a face. Can they change the appearance of their eyes—open them wide, shut them tightly, look to one side? How about their mouths—shape them into an *O*, give a toothy smile, stick out their tongues? Provide a few hand mirrors and invite children to practice making funny faces for this fun-filled class book.

Skills

❉ Concepts of print
❉ Beginning sound of *F*
❉ Sight words: *are, funny, find, here, your*

✂ Materials

● 9- by 12-inch construction paper, one per child, plus one for the cover
● several small photos of children (for cover)
● $3\frac{1}{2}$-inch square funny-face photos, three per child
● text box (page 65), one per child
● hole punch
● two metal or plastic rings (for binding)

Get Ready

Take digital photos of each child making three different funny faces. Print the photos and cut each one into a $3\frac{1}{2}$-inch square. Make a reduced copy of several of the photos for use on the cover.

Make the Cover (for teacher)

1. Label a sheet of construction paper with the title "Funny Faces."

2. Add an author line.

3. Glue the small photos around the text.

Make the Pages (*for students*)

1. Glue your three photos across one long side of a sheet of construction paper, as shown.

2. Write your name on the line of your text box (or have your teacher write it).

3. Glue the text box below your photos.

Assemble the Book

1. Stack the student pages in any order desired. Place the cover on top.

2. Punch two holes along the top edge of each page, aligning the holes in all of the pages.

3. Use two rings to bind the pages together.

Here are _____ Dante _____'s
funny faces. Find your favorite!

If desired, trim children's photos to a smaller size, then invite them to draw a frame around each one on their page.

More Letter Learning

Reduce and make additional copies of children's funny face photos (black-and-white or color). Distribute large construction-paper cutouts of the letter *F*. Then invite children to arrange and glue photos onto their letter to make a funny-face *F*. Or have them draw funny faces on the letter.

What's Growing in the Garden?

Introduce the Letter

✳ ✳ ✳

Read aloud *The Surprise Garden* by Zoe Hall (Scholastic, 1999). Afterward, point out that *garden* begins with the letter *G*. Show children a letter card labeled with an uppercase and lowercase *Gg*. Then invite youngsters to create this class book filled with some garden surprises of their own!

Skills

✳ Concepts of print
✳ Hard sound of *G*
✳ Sight words: *in, is, the, what*

✂ Materials

- 4½- by 12-inch blue construction paper, one per child, plus one for the cover
- 9- by 12-inch brown construction paper, one per child, plus one for the cover
- crayons
- magazines and catalogs
- 5- by 6-inch pieces of brown construction paper
- text box (page 66), one per child
- hole punch
- two metal or plastic rings (for binding)

Get Ready

Gather some old gardening magazines, seed catalogs, or other materials containing pictures of different fruits or vegetables grown in a garden.

Make the Cover (for teacher)

1. Follow steps 1 and 2 in Make the Pages.

2. Write the title "What's Growing in the Garden?" on the ground section of the cover.

3. Add an author line.

Make the Pages *(for students)*

1. Tear away about a one-inch strip from one long edge of your blue paper.

2. Glue the blue paper to your brown paper to make a sky and ground. Draw a yellow sun on the sky.

3. Cut out a picture of a food that is grown in a garden. Glue the picture near the bottom of your page at the middle.

4. Glue the piece of brown paper over the picture, gluing only along the left side to make a flap.

5. Draw wavy lines to look like garden rows on the ground section of the page, including on the closed flap.

6. Write your name in the text box, then glue it to the flap.

7. Open the flap and have your teacher write the name of your food on the back.

Assemble the Book

1. Stack the student pages in any order desired. Place the cover on top.

2. Punch two holes along the left edge of each page, aligning the holes in all of the pages.

3. Use two rings to bind the pages together.

Tip

Check that children have centered the flap over their picture before they glue it in place. When the flap is closed, the picture will not show, but it will appear when the flap is opened.

More Letter Learning

Challenge children to grow a letter G! Partially fill a disposable aluminum pan with potting soil. Use a pencil to draw a G in the soil. Then give children a seed for a fast-growing plant. (Lima beans work well). Have children push their seed into the soil somewhere along the imprint of the letter. Cover the seeds with soil, water them, then encourage children to care for their garden over the next few weeks as they watch for their letter to grow.

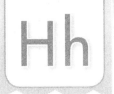

Holding Hands

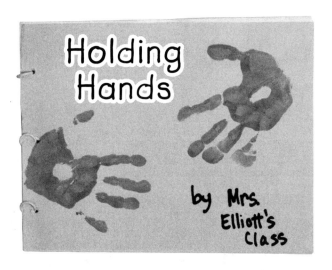

Introduce the Letter

❋ ❋ ❋

Hold up your hand and tell children that the word *hand* begins with the letter *H*. Then show them a letter card labeled with an uppercase and lowercase *Hh*. Next, ask children to take a look at their own hands. What are some things they can do with their hands? After children share their ideas, point out that hands are excellent for holding things. Finally, invite them to make this class book in which their hands can hold either realistic or silly things!

Skills

❋ Concepts of print
❋ Beginning sound of *H*
❋ Sight words: *a, her, his, in, is*

✂ Materials

- paint, in several different skin tones
- paintbrush
- two sheets of 9- by 12-inch construction paper, any color (for front and back covers)
- 9- by 12-inch white construction paper, one sheet per child
- magazines and sales flyers
- hole punch
- three metal or plastic rings (for binding)

Get Ready

Gather magazines, sales flyers, and other materials that picture a variety of things that begin with *H*.

Make the Cover (for teacher)

1. Invite a volunteer to make two paint handprints on a colored sheet of construction paper.

2. Once the paint is dry, write the title "Holding Hands" on the page.

3. Add an author line.

Make the Pages *(for students)*

1. Have your teacher paint both your palms with paint that matches your skin tone. Make a print of each hand on the center of your white paper, placing your hands so that the pinky sides touch, as shown. (This means making one print at a time, or crossing your wrists to make both prints at the same time.)

2. Wash and dry your hands.

3. Set your handprints aside to dry.

4. Cut out a magazine picture of an item that begins with *H*. Glue the picture onto your handprints so that it looks like the hands are holding the pictured item.

5. Have your teacher write this text on the page, using your name and the name of the picture: "_____ is holding _____ in his/her hands."

Assemble the Book

1. Stack the student pages in any order desired. Place the cover on top and the plain sheet of colored paper on bottom.

2. Punch three holes along the left edge of each page, aligning the holes in all of the pages.

3. Use three rings to bind the pages together.

Elise is holding honey in her hands.

Tip

You might precut a collection of pictures that begin with *H* for younger students to use on their pages.

More Letter Learning

For further discussion of hands and all they can do, read aloud Lois Ehlert's *Hands* (Harcourt Children's Books, 1997). As you read, encourage children to listen for words that begin with *H*.

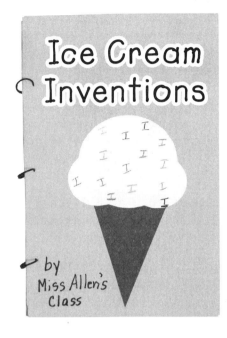

Ice Cream
Inventions

by
Miss Allen's
Class

Skills

❋ Concepts of print
❋ Long and short sounds of *I*
❋ Sight words: *an, be, I, if, it, would*

 Materials

- ice cream scoops (page 67), one per child, plus one for the cover
- brown ice cream cones (page 68), one per child, plus one for the cover
- 12- by 18-inch yellow construction paper, one sheet per child, plus one for the cover
- a variety of craft materials, such as squeeze-bottle paints, confetti, craft-foam and paper scraps, and colored cotton balls (for decorating scoops)
- text box (page 68), one per child
- hole punch
- three metal or plastic rings (for binding)

Ice Cream Inventions

Introduce the Letter

❋ ❋ ❋

Invite children to cast a vote for their favorite ice cream flavor. Which is the class favorite? After tallying up the results, point out that *ice cream* begins with the letter *I*. Show children a letter card labeled with an uppercase and lowercase *Ii*. Then ask them to imagine a new ice cream flavor—one that they would invent if they had a chance! Finally, invite them to create a page for a class book to feature their "ice cream invention."

Get Ready

Copy the ice cream scoop (page 67) on construction paper in a variety of colors. Prepare enough for each child to have one, plus an extra for the cover. Also, copy a class supply, plus one, of the ice cream cone (page 68) onto light brown construction paper.

Make the Cover (for teacher)

1. Follow steps 1 and 2 in Make the Pages. Glue the ice cream cone near the bottom of the page.

2. Write the title "Ice Cream Inventions" at the top of the page.

3. Add an author line at the bottom.

Make the Pages *(for students)*

1. Choose a color scoop that represents the ice cream you will invent.

2. Glue the scoop to a cone. Then glue the ice cream cone to the center of a sheet of yellow construction paper.

3. Decorate the scoop with one or two craft materials of your choice.

4. Glue your text box to the page above your ice cream.

5. Describe your ice cream flavor to complete the thought on the text box. Have your teacher write your dictated text at the bottom of the page.

Assemble the Book

1. Stack the student pages in any order desired. Place the cover on top.

2. Punch three holes along the left edge of each page, aligning the holes in all of the pages.

3. Use three rings to bind the pages together.

If I invented an ice cream flavor, it would be...

strawberry with chocolate chip cookie pieces.

—Ellie

To decorate the ice cream scoop on the cover, invite children to use crayons to write small versions of capital *I* all over the scoop. The colorful letters will resemble ice-cream sprinkles.

More Letter Learning

Invite children to make their own personal *I*-sprinkled ice cream cones to reinforce the long sound of *I*. Simply distribute copies of the scoop and cone, have children glue the two pieces together and then use crayons or colored pencils to "sprinkle" their scoop with capital *I* in a variety of colors.

Jack and Jill Jump

Introduce the Letter

❊ ❊ ❊

Recite the traditional nursery rhyme, "Jack and Jill." Afterward, tell children that the names *Jack* and *Jill* begin with the letter *J*. Display a letter card labeled with an uppercase and lowercase *Jj*. Then inform children that, in addition to climbing hills, Jack and Jill can also jump quite well! Invite them to make this class book in which the nursery rhyme pair leap over various items that begin with *J*.

Skills

❊ Concepts of print
❊ Beginning sound of *J*
❊ Sight words: *a, and, can, jump, over*

✂ Materials

● Jack and Jill pattern (page 69)
● 9- by 12-inch blue construction paper, one per child, plus two for the cover and title page
● green tempera paint
● plastic forks
● pictures of items that begin with *J*
● black crayons
● clear tape

Get Ready

Gather and cut out a supply of pictures that show items beginning with the letter *J*. Use magazines, as well as images printed from the Internet and your clip-art collection. Provide at least one picture for each child. Write "Jack and Jill can jump over…" on the board.

Make the Cover and Title Page (for teacher)

1. To make the cover, color, cut out, and glue the picture of Jack and Jill to a sheet of blue construction paper.

2. Write the title "Jack and Jill Jump" near the art. Add an author line.

3. For the title page, follow steps 1 and 2 in Make the Pages to create a grass line on another sheet of blue paper. Write "Jack and Jill can jump over…" above the grass line.

4. Glue the cover and title page together back-to-back.

Make the Pages *(for students)*

1. To make a line of grass (as shown below), dip the tines of a fork into green paint and press the fork repeatedly along the bottom edge of your paper.

2. Choose a picture that begins with *J*. Glue it to the center of the page along the top of the grass line.

3. Use a black crayon to make a dotted, curved line over your picture—this is a "jump" line.

4. Read the text on the board and complete the thought ("Jack and Jill can jump over…") with the name of your picture. Have your teacher write your response at the top of your page, as shown.

Tip

For added texture, glue short strips of green paper to the grassy section.

Assemble the Book

1. Place the cover facedown.

2. Use clear tape to connect the student pages to each other side by side. Tape the first student page to the title page, as shown.

3. Fold the pages back and forth, accordion-style, so that the cover is faceup on the top of the stack.

More Letter Learning

For more jumping fun, read aloud *Jump, Frog, Jump* by Robert Kalan (Perfection Learning, 2010). After enjoying the story, challenge children to jump around the room in search of words and objects that begin with *J*.

Kk

Keep
Up
Your
Kite!

by
Mrs. Carmer's Class

Keep Up Your Kite!

Introduce the Letter

✳ ✳ ✳

Show children a few pictures of kites. Point out that *kite* begins with the letter *K*. Display a letter card labeled with an uppercase and lowercase *Kk*. Then create a simple two-column chart labeled with "Yes" and "No." Write "Have you ever flown a kite?" at the top of the chart. Next, give children small paper diamond shapes. Have them add their "kite" to the appropriate column, then discuss the results. Finally, whether children have actually ever flown a kite or not, invite them to pretend to fly one in this fun class book!

Skills

✳ Concepts of print
✳ Beginning sound of *K*
✳ Sight words: *keep, up, your*

Materials

- 4- to 4½-inch white construction-paper diamonds, one per child, plus one for the cover
- 6- by 18-inch blue construction paper, one per child, plus one for the cover
- trimmed photo of each child
- colored markers
- yarn in a variety of colors
- text box (page 69), one per child
- hole punch
- two metal or plastic rings (for binding)

Get Ready

Ask children to pose in a position so they appear to be holding a kite string. Take a digital photo of each child, print it out, then trim loosely around the child's body in the picture.

Make the Cover (*for teacher*)

1. Decorate a white paper diamond, as in step 1 in Make the Pages, to make a kite.

2. Glue the kite near the top of a sheet of blue paper. Add a yarn kite string.

3. Write the title "Keep Up Your Kite!" on the page. Add an author line.

Make the Pages *(for students)*

1. To make a kite, use the markers to decorate your white paper diamond with the colors and designs of your choice.

2. Glue your kite about 4 inches from the top of your blue paper.

3. Glue your picture near the bottom of your page.

4. Cut a piece of yarn to fit between the bottom of your kite and your picture, making it long enough to curve, if desired. This is your kite string—glue it in place, as shown.

5. Write your name (or have your teacher write it) in your text box. Glue the text box to the top of your page.

Assemble the Book

1. Stack the student pages in any order desired. Place the cover on top.

2. Punch two holes along the top edge of each page, aligning the holes in all of the pages.

3. Use two rings to bind the pages together.

Keep up your kite, Marisol

Tip

You might precut the yarn into lengths from 6 to 10 inches.

More Letter Learning

Provide additional lengths of yarn, as well as any leftover pieces from the project. Ask children to use the strings to create an uppercase and lowercase *K*. As they work, encourage them to visually search the room to find words that begin with that letter.

Lovely Ladybugs

Introduce the Letter

✳ ✳ ✳

Show children the cover of *Ten Little Ladybugs* by Melanie Gerth (Piggy Toes Press, 2007). Point out that the words *ladybugs* and *little* begin with the letter *L*. Show children a letter card labeled with an uppercase and lowercase *Ll*. Then read the book aloud to get children ready for both ladybugs and counting—a perfect combination for this class-made book!

Skills

✳ Concepts of print
✳ Beginning sound of *L*
✳ Sight words: *has, little, them*
✳ Number words

✂ Materials

- tagboard templates of ladybug body (page 70)
- 9- by 12-inch black construction-paper, one per child, plus one for cover
- 12-inch squares of green construction paper, one per child, plus one for the cover
- 7-inch red construction-paper circles, one per child, plus one for the cover
- black construction paper scraps
- hole punch
- white chalk
- text box (page 71), one per child
- two metal or plastic rings (for binding)

Get Ready

Copy the ladybug body template (page 70) onto several sheets of tagboard and cut out. Also cut out a class supply (plus one) of 7-inch circles from red construction paper.

Make the Cover (*for teacher*)

1. Make a ladybug on a sheet of green construction paper, positioning it near the bottom of the page. Follow steps 1 through 5 in Make the Pages, spreading the wings to allow space for writing between them.

2. Write the title "Lovely Ladybugs" on the page.

3. Add an author line. Use chalk to write it on the ladybug body, as shown.

Make the Pages *(for students)*

1. Place the ladybug body template on a sheet of black construction paper and trace around it with chalk. Cut out the shape.

2. Glue the ladybug body to your green paper. Leave room at the bottom for the text box.

3. Cut a red circle in half. Glue the two half-circles to your ladybug to make wings, as shown.

4. Cut out two antennae from black paper scraps, then glue them to your ladybug.

5. Punch out some black dots with a hole punch. Glue them to the wings.

6. Count the dots. Then have your teacher complete a text box by filling in your name and the number of dots on your ladybug. Glue the text box to the bottom of the page.

Assemble the Book

1. Stack the student pages in any order desired. Place the cover on top.

2. Punch two holes along the left edge of each page, aligning the holes in all of the pages.

3. Use two rings to bind the pages together.

_____ Tori _____ 's lovely ladybug
has _____ six _____ little dots. Count them.

Tips

✳ If desired, provide wiggle eyes for children to add to their ladybugs.

✳ Instead of using a hole-punch, die-cut a supply of black circles for children to use on their ladybug wings.

More Letter Learning

For additional practice with this letter sound, invite children to turn to any page in the class book. Have them name a different word that begins with *L* as they point to each dot on the ladybug.

Meet Our Monsters!

❈ ❈ ❈

Show children the cover of *Go Away, Big Green Monster!* by Ed Emberley (Little, Brown and Company, 1992). Point out that *monster* begins with the letter *M*. Show children a letter card labeled with an uppercase and lowercase *Mm*. Then read the book aloud. Afterward, ask children if the monster in the story was scary. Are all monsters scary? Can they be cute? Silly? Finally, invite children to craft their own monsters for this class book featuring the letter *M*.

Skills

❈ Concepts of print
❈ Beginning sound of *M*
❈ Sight words: *my, our*

 ## Materials

- 9- by 12-inch construction paper, one per child, plus one for the cover
- tempera paint in a variety of colors
- wiggle or sticker eyes in various sizes
- a variety of craft materials, such as buttons, pom-poms, coffee filters, and pipe cleaners
- colored markers
- hole punch
- two metal or plastic rings (for binding)

Get Ready

Prepare several cups of tempera paint in different colors. Provide a wide paintbrush or plastic spoon for each paint container.

Make the Cover (for teacher)

1. Write the title "Meet Our Monsters!" on a sheet of construction paper.

2. Put a few colorful blobs of paint around the title.

3. Allow the paint to dry. Then convert the blobs into monsters by adding wiggle or sticker eyes and drawing on features with markers.

4. Add an author line.

Make the Pages *(for students)*

1. Choose a sheet of construction paper in the color of your choice. Then choose paint in a different color.

2. Put a few blobs of paint in the center of your paper. Fold the paper in half. Then slide your hand firmly across the paper from the fold outward to spread the paint.

3. Unfold the paper to see the resulting paint shape. Allow the paint to dry.

4. Transform your paint shape into a monster face! Glue on craft items of your choice, including one or more wiggle eyes (or affix sticker eyes). If you wish, use a marker to add other features—such as ears, eyes, or antennae.

5. Choose a name that begins with *M* for your monster. Have your teacher write "Meet my monster, _____" on your page, using the name of your monster to complete the sentence.

Meet my monster, Marty.

Assemble the Book

1. Stack the student pages in any order desired. Place the cover on top.

2. Punch two holes along the top edge of each page, aligning the holes in all of the pages.

3. Use two rings to bind the pages together.

For textured monsters, add sand or salt to the paint.

More Letter Learning

After sharing the class book once or twice as written, read it aloud once again. This time, as you read each child's page, ask that child to tell about a food—real or silly—that begins with *M* that his or her monster might like to eat. For example, a child might say, "My monster, Molly, might like marshmallows" or "My monster, Manfred, munches motorcycles."

Nn

Near at Night

❋ ❋ ❋

Give children a clue about the setting of this night-related class book by dimming the classroom lights and shining a flashlight around the darkened room. Ask children to guess what time of day your class book will feature (*night*). Once they guess, tell them that *night* begins with the letter *N*, then shine the flashlight on a letter card labeled with an uppercase and lowercase *Nn*.

Skills

❋ Concepts of print
❋ Beginning sound of *N*
❋ Sight words: *a, but, did, it, not, one, only, was*

✂ Materials

● 9- by 12-inch black construction paper, one per child, plus one for the cover
● 7-inch gray paper circle (for the cover)
● trimmed photo of each child
● pictures of items that begin with *N*
● 4- by 5-inch black construction paper, one per child
● text box (page 71), one per child
● white art pencil or crayon
● star stickers
● hole punch
● two metal or plastic rings (for binding)

Get Ready

Take a head-and-shoulder digital photo of each child. Print a small image of each photo (in color or in black and white), then trim loosely around the child in each picture. Also, gather and cut out a supply of pictures that show items beginning with the letter *N*. Use magazines, as well as images printed from the Internet and your clip-art collection.

Make the Cover (for teacher)

1. Label the gray circle with the title "Near at Night."

2. Add markings to the circle to make it resemble the moon. Then glue the circle to the center of a sheet of black construction paper.

3. Use the white art pencil (or crayon) to add an author line to the page.

Make the Pages *(for students)*

1. Glue a text box to the top of your page, as shown.

2. Glue your photo to the left side of your black paper near the bottom.

3. Choose a picture that begins with *N*. Glue it to the right side of your paper near the bottom.

4. Glue the smaller piece of black paper over the *N* picture, gluing only along the left side to make a flap.

5. Ask your teacher to write the name of the *N* picture in white on the back of the flap. Then write your name in the text box (or have your teacher write it).

6. Add star stickers to the black areas of your page, including the flap, to make it look like a night sky.

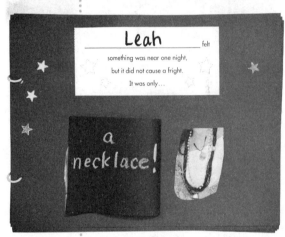

Assemble the Book

1. Stack the student pages in any order desired. Place the cover on top.

2. Punch two holes along the left edge of each page, aligning the holes in all of the pages.

3. Use two rings to bind the pages together.

Tip

Check that children have centered the flap over their *N* picture before they glue it in place. When the flap is closed, the picture will not show, but it will appear when the flap is opened.

More Letter Learning

Reinforce the letter-sound connection by giving children a large letter *N* cut from black construction paper. Then have them decorate their letter with foil star stickers, as well as a small, yellow, construction-paper crescent moon. As they work, remind children that *N* is for *night*!

On and Off the Ovals

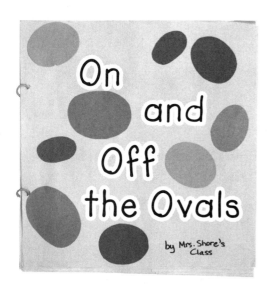

✳ ✳ ✳

Review the positional concepts of *on* and *off* with children. To begin, point out that both of these words begin with the letter *O*. Display a letter card labeled with an uppercase and lowercase *Oo*. Then give a command featuring *on* or *off* for each child to follow, such as "Put your hands *on* your knees," or "Take one foot *off* the rug." Afterward, invite children to show off their knowledge of these concepts—and the letter *O*—by making this class book.

Skills

✳ Concepts of print

✳ Long and short sounds of O

✳ Sight words: *is, off, on, the*

 ## Materials

- 12-inch squares of white construction paper, one per child, plus one for the cover
- several ovals in various sizes and colors (for the cover)
- $3\frac{1}{2}$-inch construction-paper ovals in various colors, one colored pair per child
- trimmed photos of each child
- text boxes (page 72), one of each per child
- hole punch
- two metal or plastic rings (for binding)

Get Ready

Take a full-body digital photo of each child. Print out two copies of each picture, then trim loosely around the child in each picture.

Make the Cover (for teacher)

1. Use the black marker to write the title "On and Off the Ovals" on a 12-inch square of white construction paper.

2. Add an author line.

3. Glue several 1-inch and 2-inch ovals on the page around the text.

Make the Pages *(for students)*

1. Glue the text box labeled "_____ is on the oval" to the bottom left side of your white paper. Glue the other text box to the bottom right side.

2. Choose two ovals of the same color. Glue an oval above each text box, as shown.

3. Glue on one of your photos so that it looks as if you are standing *on* the left oval.

4. Glue your other photo next to the right oval so that it looks as if you are *off* the oval.

5. Write your name in each text box (or have your teacher write it).

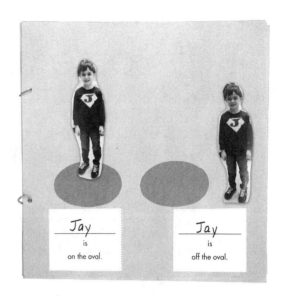

Assemble the Book

1. Stack the student pages in any order desired. Place the cover on top.

2. Punch two holes along the left edge of each page, aligning the holes in all of the pages.

3. Use two rings to bind the pages together.

Tip

In advance, glue the text boxes to the bottom of each child's page to ensure they are placed correctly.

More Letter Learning

Explore more *opposites*—and this additional word that begins with *O*—by reading aloud *You and Me: We're Opposites* by Harriet Ziefert (Blue Apple Books, 2009). After sharing the book, work with children to generate a list of words that begin with *O*. Finally, review the words and sort them according to whether they begin with the long- or the short-vowel sound of *O*.

Put Some on My Plate, Please!

Skills

* Concepts of print
* Beginning sound of *P*
* Sight words: *my, on, please, put, some*

✂ Materials

* 9-inch white paper plates, one per child, plus one for the cover
* text box (page 72), one per child
* crayons
* hole punch
* one metal or plastic ring (for binding)

Introduce the Letter

✳ ✳ ✳

Write the word *pizza* on a sheet of chart paper. Point out that this word begins with the letter *P*. Display a letter card labeled with an uppercase and lowercase *Pp*. Then work with children to brainstorm a list of other foods that begin with *P*, such as *popcorn, pasta, pickles, pears, peaches, pineapple, pumpkins, pretzels, pitas, pork chops, pepperoni, pie,* and *pudding*. Write the words on the chart paper. Finally, invite children to make this class book.

Get Ready

Display the list of food names that begin with *P* in a prominent place so children can easily refer to it as they make their book page.

Make the Cover (for teacher)

1. Use the black marker to write the title "Put Some on My Plate, Please!" on a paper plate.

2. Add an author line.

3. Draw a few pictures of foods that begin with *P* around the text.

Make the Pages *(for students)*

1. Choose a food that begins with *P* from the class list.

2. Draw this food in the center of your paper plate.

3. Write the name of the food on your text box (or ask your teacher to write it). Then glue the text box near the bottom rim of your plate.

4. Have your teacher write "_____ says," at the top rim of your plate (as shown), using your name to complete the phrase.

Assemble the Book

1. Stack the student pages in any order desired. Place the cover on top.

2. Punch a hole in the top rim of each page, aligning the holes in all of the pages.

3. Use the ring to bind the pages together.

If desired, write the text at the top rim of children's plates before they create their pages.

More Letter Learning

The focus on so many yummy foods that begin with *P* is bound to make children's mouths water! To satisfy their cravings, serve up a sweet-and-salty treat of pudding and pretzel sticks. Simply put some pudding on a paper plate with pretzel sticks to the side. Before children eat their snack, encourage them to draw a *P* in the pudding using a pretzel-stick "pencil."

Note: Be sure to check in advance for any food allergies.

What Is Quiet?

Introduce the Letter

✳ ❄ ✳

Show children the cover of *The Very Quiet Cricket* by Eric Carle (Philomel, 1990). point out that the word *quiet* begins with the letter *Q*. Show children a letter card labeled with an uppercase and lowercase *Qq*. Then read the story aloud. After enjoying this classic story, invite children to brainstorm other things that are very quiet. Now they're set to create this simple class book!

Skills

✳ Concepts of print
✳ Beginning sound of Q
✳ Sight words: *a, is*

Materials

- 9- by 12-inch construction paper, one sheet per child, plus one for the cover
- white construction-paper clouds
- magazines, catalogs, and sales flyers
- text box (page 73)
- hole punch
- two metal or plastic rings (for binding)

Get Ready

Gather magazines, catalogs, sales flyers, or other materials containing pictures of things that are quiet, such as furniture, foods, and clothes. Also, cut out a few white cloud shapes in different sizes to use on the cover.

Make the Cover *(for teacher)*

1. Write the title "What Is Quiet?" on a white construction-paper cloud cutout.

2. Label another cloud cutout with an author line.

3. Glue the labeled clouds to a sheet of construction paper, adding a few other cloud cutouts if desired.

Make the Pages *(for students)*

1. Look through a magazine, catalog, or sales flyer to find a picture of something that is quiet. Cut out the picture.

2. Glue the picture to the center of your paper.

3. Have your teacher write the name of the picture in your text box. Glue the text box above or below the picture on your page.

A _sandwich_ is quiet.

—Josh

Assemble the Book

1. Stack the student pages in any order desired. Place the cover on top.

2. Punch two holes along the left edge of each page, aligning the holes in all of the pages.

3. Use two rings to bind the pages together.

Tip

You might precut a collection of pictures of things that are quiet for younger students to use on their pages.

More Letter Learning

Arrange to have some quiet, letter-focused time in your classroom. To begin, write the word *quiet* on the board and remind children that this word begins with Q. Then give them a sheet of paper with a large, block-letter Q drawn on it. Explain that they will decorate their Q with watercolor paints as they listen to some quiet, soothing music (e.g., a new age recording or soft classical piece).

Our Rectangle Robots

Introduce the Letter

✳ ✳ ✳

Show children a variety of paper shape cutouts, including a circle, square, triangle, and rectangle. Have them identify each shape. Then ask them which shape begins with the sound of the letter *R* (*rectangle*). After children identify the rectangle, show them a letter card labeled with an uppercase and lowercase *Rr*. Finally, explain that children will make a book filled with robots made only of rectangles.

Skills

✳ Concepts of print
✳ Beginning sound of *R*
✳ Sight word: *is*

✂ Materials

- 12- by 18-inch construction paper, one sheet per child, plus one for the cover
- construction-paper rectangles in various colors and sizes
- text box (page 73), one per child
- hole punch
- three metal or plastic rings (for binding)

Get Ready

Cut a large supply of construction-paper rectangles in a variety of colors and sizes. (Include sizes that can be used for robot bodies, arms, legs, buttons, eyes, mouths, and so on.)

Make the Cover (for teacher)

1. Write the title "Our Rectangle Robots" on a sheet of construction paper.

2. Add an author line.

3. Glue several rectangles to the cover around the text.

Make the Pages *(for students)*

1. Glue your text box to the top of your page.

2. Choose a few rectangles to use for your robot's head and body. Arrange these on your page, then glue them in place.

3. Add more rectangles to your robot to make features such as eyes, ears, arms, feet, and so on. Glue the rectangles in place as you work. (If needed, trim some of the rectangles to fit your design, but make sure they still keep a rectangle shape.)

4. Choose a name that begins with letter *R* for your robot. (You can use a real or silly name.)

5. Have your teacher write your name and your robot's name in the text box.

Assemble the Book

1. Stack the student pages in any order desired. Place the cover on top.

2. Punch three holes along the left edge of each page, aligning the holes in all of the pages.

3. Use three rings to bind the pages together.

Tip

In advance, assemble a rectangle robot on a sheet of construction paper. Display the page as a model for children as they create their own rectangle robots.

More Letter Learning

After reading through the class book a couple of times, read it once more. This time, as you read each child's page, ask that child to name an item or activity that begins with *R* that his or her robot might like. For example, read the text "Charlie's rectangle robot is named Ricky. He likes…" and have the child add his response, such as "rodeos!"

Silly Soup

Silly Soup

by
Miss Caldwell's
Class

Introduce the Letter

❊ ❊ ❊

Write the word *soup* on the board. Point out that this word begins with the letter *S*. Then display a letter card labeled with an uppercase and lowercase *Ss*. Next, invite children to tell about their favorite kinds of soup. No doubt, they'll mention child favorites, such as chicken noodle, tomato, or alphabet soup. Finally, explain to children that they will create a class book full of their own silly soup concoctions in which all of the ingredients begin with or represent the letter *S*!

Skills

❊ Concepts of print
❊ Beginning sound of *S*
❊ Sight words *and, is, made, with*

 ## Materials

- copy of soup bowl (page 74) with text masked (for the cover)
- colorful copies of the soup bowl and soup patterns (pages 74–75), one of each per child, plus one soup pattern for the cover
- variety of craft items that represent the letter *S* or *S* words
- hole punch
- two metal or plastic rings (for binding)

Get Ready

Gather a variety of craft materials that begin with *S*, such as sequins, straws, string, stickers, stamps, shapes (cut from paper or craft foam), sand (in different colors), and sunflower seeds. You might also include materials that have an *S* shape or represent words that begin with *S*, such as stickers of snowflakes, stars, seahorses, spiders, and suns. Also, make construction paper copies of the soup bowl and soup patterns (pages 74–75) in a variety of colors.

Make the Cover *(for teacher)*

1. Follow step 1 in Make the Pages. Use the soup bowl with the text masked for the cover.

2. Write the title "Silly Soup!" on the soup cutout. Add craft materials to represent soup ingredients, as in step 2 in Make the Pages.

3. Add an author line to the bowl.

Make the Pages *(for students)*

1. Cut out a soup bowl and soup pattern. Glue the soup to the bowl.

2. Choose two different craft items to use as ingredients of your soup. Glue the items to the soup part of your page.

3. Have your teacher complete the text box with your name and the name of your soup ingredients, using words that begin with *S* to describe the ingredients.

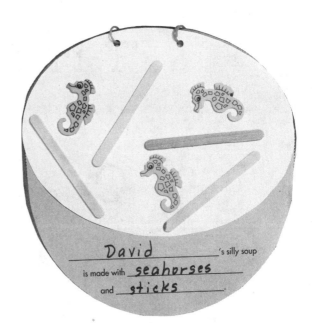

David's silly soup is made with seahorses and sticks.

Assemble the Book

1. Stack the student pages in any order desired. Place the cover on top.

2. Punch two holes along the top edge of each page, aligning the holes in all of the pages.

3. Use two rings to bind the pages together.

Tip

If desired, cut out the soup bowl and soup patterns in advance. You also might glue each soup cutout to a bowl.

More Letter Learning

Serve up some not-so-silly alphabet soup at snack time. Ask children to try to find at least one *S* in their bowl. Once they find the letter, challenge them to find a word or item in the room that begins with *S*.

Note: Be sure to check in advance for any food allergies.

"T-rrific" Tents

Introduce the Letter

❄ ❄ ❄

Drape a blanket or sheet over a table to create a makeshift tent in your classroom. Then place several items in it that begin with the letter *T*, such as a toy tiger, towel, toothbrush, tape, telephone, and a number card with *10* printed on it. Invite children to go inside the tent two at a time to explore the items. After everyone has had a turn, ask children to tell what all the items in the tent have in common *(they all start with the letter* T*)*. Show children a letter card labeled with an uppercase and lowercase *Tt*. Finally, invite them to make this tent-themed class book filled with items that begin with *T*.

Skills

❄ Concepts of print
❄ Beginning sound of *T*
❄ Sight words: *in, is, what*

Materials

- tent (page 76) with text masked (for the cover)
- colorful construction-paper copies of tent (page 76), one per child
- plain, white copy paper
- magazines, catalogs, and sales flyers
- crayons
- hole punch
- two metal or plastic rings (for binding)

Get Ready

Gather magazines, catalogs, sales flyers, or other materials containing pictures of things that begin with *T*. Also, duplicate the tent pattern (page 76) onto colored construction paper for each child. Then mask the text and make another copy for the cover.

Make the Cover *(for teacher)*

1. Cut out the tent pattern with the masked text. Write this title on the cutout: "T-rrific" Tents.

2. Add an author line to the page.

3. If desired, cut an additional sheet of construction paper in the shape of the tent to use as a back cover.

Make the Pages (for students)

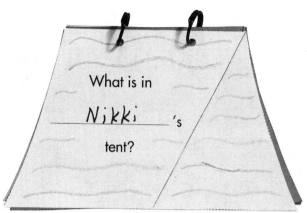

1. Cut out the tent pattern (with text) and write your name on the blank line (or have your teacher write it).

2. Use crayons to decorate your tent as desired.

3. Fold back the flap of your tent. Then glue your tent to a sheet of white copy paper. Do not glue down the flap.

4. Close the flap, then trim the white paper to the shape or your tent.

5. Look through a magazine, catalog, or sales flyer to find a picture of something that begins with *T*. Cut out the picture and glue it to the white paper under the flap.

6. Have your teacher write the name of the item under the picture (or on the back of the flap).

Assemble the Book

1. Stack the student pages in any order desired. Place the cover on top. (Add a back cover, if desired.)

2. Punch two holes along the top edge of each page, aligning the holes in all of the pages.

3. Use two rings to bind the pages together.

Tips

❋ Check that the picture fits under the flap. When the flap is closed, the picture will not show, but it will appear when the flap is opened.

❋ If desired, precut a supply of tent shapes from white copy paper for students to glue to the back of their tent cutouts.

More Letter Learning

Read the class-made book with children. Record the *T*-word pictured on each page on chart paper. After reading, review the list of words with children. Then ask them, as a class, to come up with at least ten more words that begin with *T* without repeating any on the list. Add their responses to the list.

Note: Be sure to check in advance for any food allergies.

Uh-Oh! We're Upside-Down!

Skills

❋ Concepts of print
❋ Long and short sounds of U
❋ Sight word: *down, is*

✂ Materials

- 9- by 12-inch construction paper, one sheet per child, plus one for the cover
- a few reduced photos of children for the cover (see Get Ready)
- black crayons
- trimmed photo of each child
- text box (page 77), one per child
- hole punch
- two metal or plastic rings (for binding)

Introduce the Letter

❋ ❋ ❋

Read aloud *Silly Sally* by Audrey Wood (Harcourt Children's Books, 1992). Do your youngsters think they'd like to walk around upside-down and backwards? After they discuss the idea, write the word *upside-down* on the board and point out that *upside* begins with the letter *U*. Show children a letter card labeled with an uppercase and lowercase *Uu*. Then invite them to make this class book where it appears they are upside-down. How silly!

Get Ready

Take a full-body, digital photo of each child standing with legs apart and arms up, in a letter *X* formation. Have them flatten their hands, palms up and with fingers pointed outward. Print out the photos and trim loosely around the child in each picture. Prepare a few extra reduced photos for use on the cover.

Make the Cover (for teacher)

1. Write the title "Uh-Oh! We're Upside-Down!" on a sheet of construction paper.

2. Glue on a few photos of children, positioning them upside-down around the text.

3. Add an author line.

Make the Pages *(for students)*

1. Use a black crayon to draw a floor line a few inches above the bottom of your paper.

2. Glue your photo, upside-down, to the paper, so it appears you are standing on your hands. Place the hands on or below the floor line.

3. Draw a door, windows, or furniture to make the scene look like the inside of a room.

4. Write your name on the text box (or have your teacher write it).

5. Glue the text box to the top of your page.

Assemble the Book

1. Stack the student pages in any order desired. Place the cover on top.

2. Punch two holes along the left edge of each page, aligning the holes in all of the pages.

3. Use two rings to bind the pages together.

Tip

Instead of drawing the interior room features, let children cut out magazine pictures of windows, doors, and furniture to glue to their pages.

More Letter Learning

Reduce the size of children's upside-down photos and copy them in black-and-white. Then distribute large construction-paper cutouts of the letter *U*. Have children glue their small upside-down photos to their letter, reminding them that *U* is for *upside-down*. Finally, challenge children to name other words that begin with *U*, such as *under*, *umpire*, *umbrella*, *unicorn*, and *universe*. Talk about whether each word has the long-vowel or short-vowel sound of *U*.

Vv

A Very Strange Vine

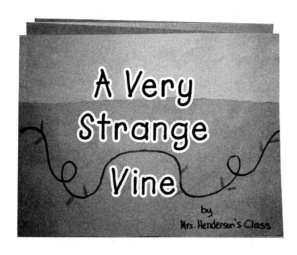

Introduce the Letter

�֍ ✤ ✤

Ask children if they can name some things that grow on a vine. Pumpkins, grapes, and melons are all good examples. Then ask, "What about valentines? Or vests?" After your giggling class corrects you, tell them that the words you just mentioned—*vines, valentines* and *vests*—both begin with the letter *V*. Next, show children a letter card labeled with an uppercase and lowercase *Vv*. Finally, tell children that they will make a class book in which some odd items do grow on a vine—a vine full of *V* words!

Skills

✤ Concepts of print
✤ Beginning sound of *V*
✤ Sight words: *a, on, one, saw, the, very, was*

✂ Materials

- 4- by 12-inch blue construction paper, one per child, plus two for the cover and title page
- 9- by 12-inch green construction paper, one sheet per child, plus two for the cover and title page
- crayons
- leaf pattern (page 77), one copy for the title page
- pictures of items that begin with *V*
- clear tape

Get Ready

Gather and cut out a supply of pictures that show items that begin with *V*, such as a vase, van, vest, valentine, vinegar, vine, and vacuum. Use magazines, as well as images printed from the Internet and your clip-art collection.

Make the Cover and Title Page
(for teacher)

1. For both the cover and title page, follow steps 1–3 in Make the Pages.

2. Write the title "A Very Strange Vine" on the cover.

3. Add an author line.

4. Write your name on the leaf pattern to complete the text. Color the leaf, then glue it to the vine on the title page.

5. Glue the cover and title page together back-to-back.

Make the Pages *(for students)*

1. Tear away about a one-inch strip from one long edge of your blue paper.

2. Glue the blue paper to your green paper to make a sky and ground.

3. Use the black crayon to draw a curvy or looping vine across the green section, as shown. Add small green leaves to the vine.

4. Choose an item that begins with *V* and glue it to your vine.

5. Have your teacher add text to your page, including the *V* word that names your picture, as shown.

After assembling the book, use a black crayon to connect the vines at the edges of the pages.

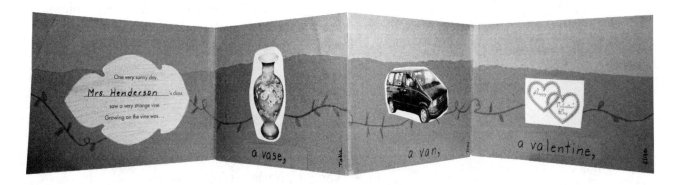

Assemble the Book

1. Place the cover facedown.

2. Use clear tape to connect the student pages to each other side by side. Tape the first student page to the title page, as shown.

3. Fold the pages back and forth, accordion-style, so that the cover is faceup on the top of the stack.

More Letter Learning

Combine motor skills and letter-sound associations with this fun follow-up. Tape a green masking-tape "vine" to the floor in an open area. Invite children to walk along the vine (like a balance beam), naming words that begin with *V* as they go.

We Want Waffles!

✳ ❋ ✳

Take a quick poll to find out which children like better for breakfast: pancakes or waffles. After sharing the results, point out that *waffles* begins with the letter *W*. Display a letter card labeled with an uppercase and lowercase *Ww*. Then tell children that whether they prefer waffles or not, they're sure to enjoy making this waffle book!

Skills

✳ Concepts of print
✳ Beginning sound of *W*
✳ Sight words: *a, want, we, with*

 ## Materials

- $\frac{3}{4}$-inch wide masking tape grid (see Get Ready)
- half-sheets of white copy paper, one per child, plus one for the cover
- unwrapped brown crayons
- 9-inch white paper plates, one per child, plus one for the cover
- craft items (for waffle toppings)
- hole punch
- one metal or plastic ring (for binding)

Get Ready

Use $\frac{3}{4}$-inch wide strips of masking tape to create a grid on a tabletop, about six inches in width and length. (The grid will have a basket-weave pattern.) Then gather a variety of craft materials children can use to represent waffle toppings, such as a squeeze-bottle of brownish-gold paint (for syrup), cotton balls (for whipped cream), and red or blue construction paper scraps (to make berries).

Make the Cover (*for teacher*)

1. Follow steps 1 and 2 in Make the Pages to create a waffle.

2. Glue the waffle to a paper plate.

3. Write the title "We Want Waffles!" on the plate.

4. Add an author line.

Make the Pages *(for students)*

1. Lay your half-sheet of paper on top of the masking-tape grid. Use the side of the brown crayon to make a crayon rubbing of the grid on your paper. When finished, your paper will have a waffle-like look.

2. Trim your paper to make a rectangular or round waffle that fits on the center of your paper plate.

3. Glue the waffle to the center of the plate.

4. Use craft materials to create a topping of your choice for your waffle. Add the topping to the waffle.

5. Have your teacher write "_____ wants a waffle with _____" on your plate (as shown), using your name at the beginning of the sentence and the name of your topping at the end.

Assemble the Book

1. Stack the student pages in any order desired. Place the cover on top.

2. Punch a hole on the left rim of each page, aligning the holes in all of the pages.

3. Use the ring to bind the pages together.

Tessa wants a waffle
with blueberries.

Tip

If desired, write the text across the top of children's plates before they create their pages. Then fill in the text at the bottom after their pages are completed.

More Letter Learning

Make some waffles for your class! Before serving the snack, squirt a syrup *W* onto a paper plate for each child. If desired, provide a few toppings for children to add to their waffles. As children enjoy their snack, encourage them to name words other than *waffle* that begin with *W*.

Note: Be sure to check in advance for any food allergies.

Excellent X-rays

Show children a photo or a real x-ray of a hand. Point out how the film is black and the bones appear in white. Then help children identify the bones in the x-ray. Afterward, point out that *x-ray* begins with the letter *X*. Display a letter card labeled with an uppercase and lowercase *Xx*. Finally, tell children that they will make imitation x-rays of their own for this class book featuring the letter *X*.

Skills

✳ Concepts of print
✳ Beginning sound of *X*
✳ Sight words: *an, of, what*

✄ Materials

- large photos of students
- 9- by 12-inch red construction paper, one per child, plus one for the cover
- 9- by 12-inch black construction paper (for the cover)
- white crayons
- 3-inch squares of black construction paper, one per child
- text box (page 78), one per child
- hole punch
- two metal or plastic rings (for binding)

Get Ready

Take a head-and-shoulders digital photo of children, having them hold up one hand with the fingers spread. Print out a black-and-white or color image of each child's photo on $8\frac{1}{2}$- by 11-inch copy paper.

Make the Cover (for teacher)

1. Trace around your hand on the black construction paper. Cut out the hand shape and glue it to a sheet of red construction paper.

2. Use a white crayon to draw the bones of your hand so that the cutout resembles an x-ray.

3. Write the title "Excellent X-rays" on the page.

4. Add an author line.

Make the Pages *(for students)*

1. Glue your photo to your red paper.

2. Glue the black square over your hand in the photo, as shown.

3. Use a white crayon to draw the bones of your hand, so the black square resembles an x-ray.

4. Write your name in the text box (or have your teacher write it).

5. Glue the text box to the bottom of your page.

What an excellent x-ray of
Vivi 's hand!

Assemble the Book

1. Stack the student pages in any order desired. Place the cover on top.

2. Punch two holes along the left edge of each page, aligning the holes in all of the pages.

3. Use two rings to bind the pages together.

Tip

Demonstrate to children how to draw the bones of their hand to resemble an x-ray.

More Letter Learning

Print a very large, bold, black *X* on a sheet of paper. (Use your computer, if desired.) Distribute copies of the letter. Then have children use a white crayon to trace their *X*, as if they are drawing the "bones" to create an x-ray of the letter!

Yummy or Yucky?

Introduce the Letter

❉　❉　❉

Draw a happy (yummy) face and a sad (yucky) face on the opposite sides of the board and write the words *yummy* and *yucky* under each corresponding picture. Point out that both words begin with the letter *Y*. Show children a letter card labeled with an uppercase and lowercase *Yy*. Then name foods one at a time, including some that children may or may not like. After naming each food, ask children to point to the yummy face and imitate that expression if they like the food. If they dislike the food, have them do the same for the yucky face. Finally, invite children to make this book filled with yummy—and yucky—foods!

Skills

❉ Concepts of print
❉ Beginning sound of Y
❉ Sight words: *does*, *like*, *not*

✂ Materials

- 9- by 12-inch construction paper, one sheet per child
- magazines and sales flyers
- text boxes (page 78), one of each per child
- hole punch
- two metal or plastic rings (for binding)

Get Ready

Gather food-related magazines and grocery store sales flyers that picture a variety of foods.

Make the Cover (for teacher)

1. Label a sheet of construction paper with the title "Yummy or Yucky?"

2. Draw a "yummy" and "yucky" face by the corresponding words.

3. Add an author line.

Make the Pages *(for students)*

1. Glue the text box that begins with "Yum!" to the bottom left side of your paper. Glue the other text box to the bottom right side.

2. Look through the magazines and sales flyers to find a picture of one food you think is yummy and one food you think is yucky.

3. Glue your yummy food above the text box on the left side of your paper.

4. Glue your yucky food above the text box on the right side.

5. Have your teacher write your name and the name of the food in each text box.

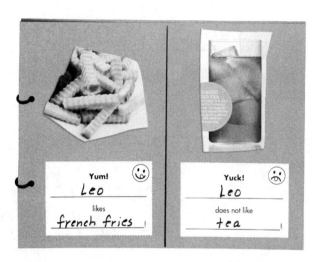

Assemble the Book

1. Stack the student pages in any order desired. Place the cover on top.

2. Punch two holes along the left edge of each page, aligning the holes in all of the pages.

3. Use two rings to bind the pages together.

To provide a placement guide for text boxes and pictures, draw a line down the middle of each child's page to divide it in half. Or, glue the text boxes to children's pages in advance.

More Letter Learning

Invite children to paint a picture of their favorite yummy food. Then have them use a paintbrush to write (or trace) the word *yummy* below their picture. What a fun way to practice forming the letter Y!

Zero Zebras at the Zoo

Introduce the Letter

❋ ❋ ❋

Show children the cover of *1, 2, 3 to the Zoo* by Eric Carle (Puffin Books, 1998). Point to the word *zoo* and tell children that it begins with the letter *Z*. Show children a letter card labeled with an uppercase and lowercase *Zz*. Then read the story aloud. This story is sure to get children in the mood to make a class book that features both zoo animals and numbers.

Skills

❋ Concepts of print
❋ Beginning sound of *Z*
❋ Sight words: *and, at, has, the*
❋ Number words

Materials

- 12- by 18-inch light blue construction paper, one sheet per child, plus one for the cover
- zebra (page 80), one copy for the cover
- crayons
- supply of zoo animals (pages 79–80), except the zebra
- text box (page 80), one per child
- hole punch
- three metal or plastic rings (for binding)

Get Ready

Make a large supply of all of the zoo animal patterns (pages 79–80) except the zebra. For this book, children may use up to five or six animals in any combination to make their pages. Make only one copy of the zebra for use on the cover.

Make the Cover (*for teacher*)

1. Write the title "Zero Zebras at the Zoo" on a sheet of construction paper.

2. Color, cut out, and glue the zebra to the page. Draw a thought bubble above the zebra and label it with "Where did we all go?"

3. Add an author line.

Make the Pages *(for students)*

1. Use a green crayon to draw a "roller coaster" line along the bottom part of your blue paper, as shown. Leave about four inches of space above the line at the top of the page.

2. Color the area below the line green to represent grass. This page represents your zoo.

3. Choose five or six zoo animal patterns. Color and cut out the animals.

4. Glue the animal cutouts to the grassy area of your zoo.

5. Have your teacher write your name in the text box. Then dictate the number and kinds of animals in your zoo so your teacher can fill in the text box.

6. Glue the text box to the top of your page.

Assemble the Book

1. Stack the student pages in any order desired. Place the cover on top.

2. Punch three holes in the left side of each page, aligning the holes in all of the pages.

3. Use the three rings to bind the pages together.

Tip

For added texture, invite children to glue short strips of green paper to the grassy area of their page.

More Letter Learning

Reduce and copy a supply of the zebra pattern on page 80. (Make enough for each child to have three or four zebras.) Then give children a construction paper cutout of a large letter *Z*. Have them color, cut out, and glue a few zebras to their *Z*. As they work, encourage children to name other words that begin with *Z*, such as *zipper, zoom, zigzag,* and *zucchini*.

_____ has a boo-boo

on his _____.

He put on a bandaid to make it better!

_____ has a boo-boo

on his _____.

He put on a bandaid to make it better!

_____ has a boo-boo

on her _____.

She put on a bandaid to make it better!

_____ has a boo-boo

on her _____.

She put on a bandaid to make it better!

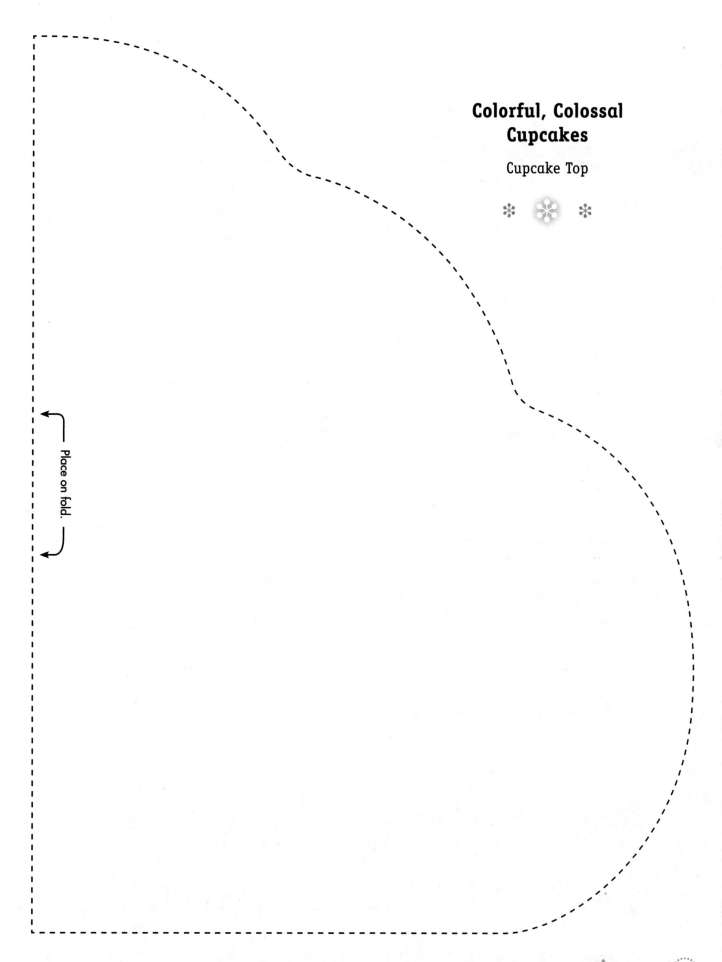

Colorful, Colossal Cupcakes

Cupcake Top

Place on fold.

Place on fold.

**Colorful, Colossal
Cupcakes**

Cupcake Bottom
and Text Box

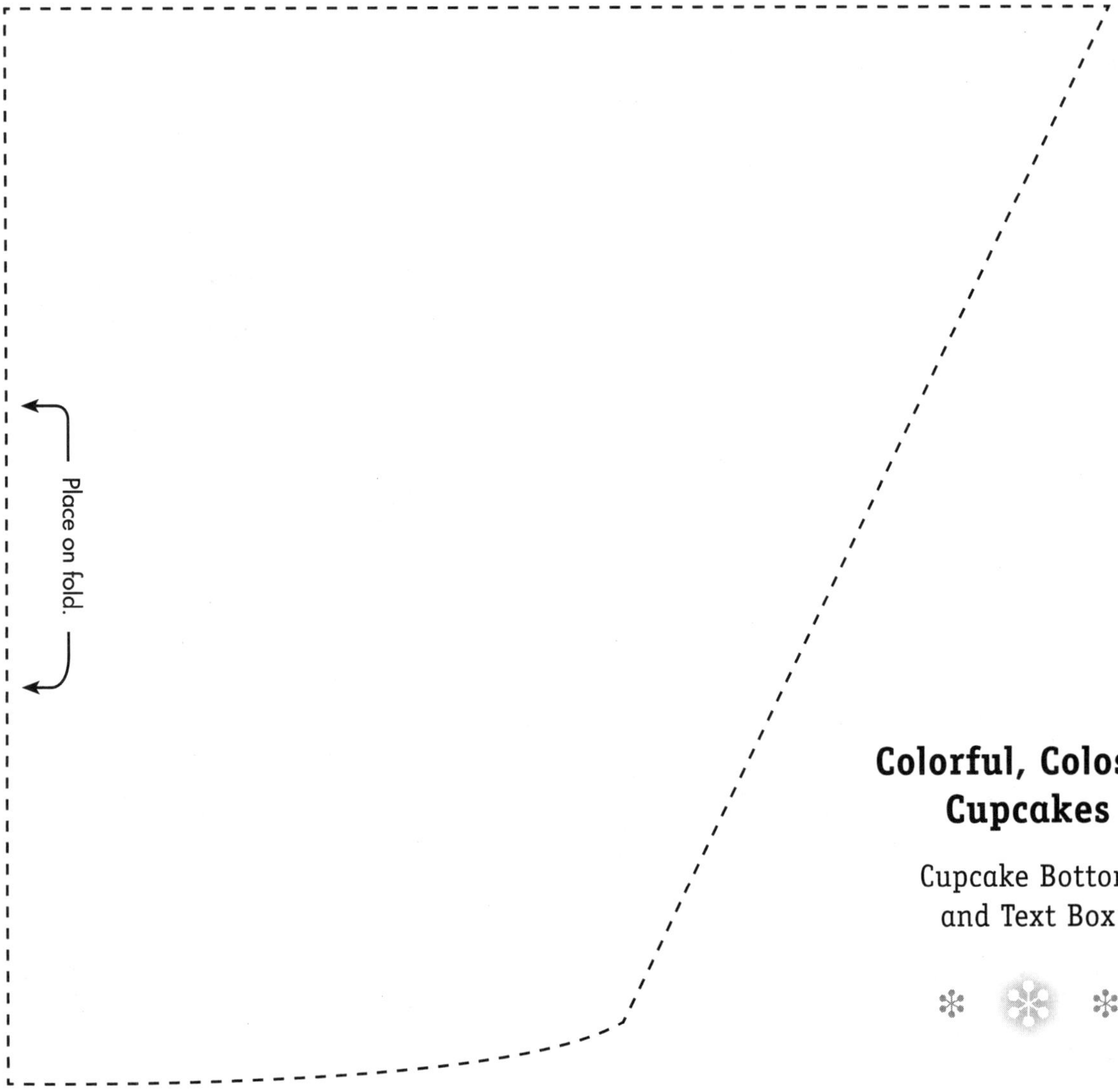

✳ ✳ ✳

_____'s

colossal cupcake is

the color _____.

This cupcake has

_____ confetti.

Ding-dong! Who's at the door?

It's

with a ___.

Fold here.

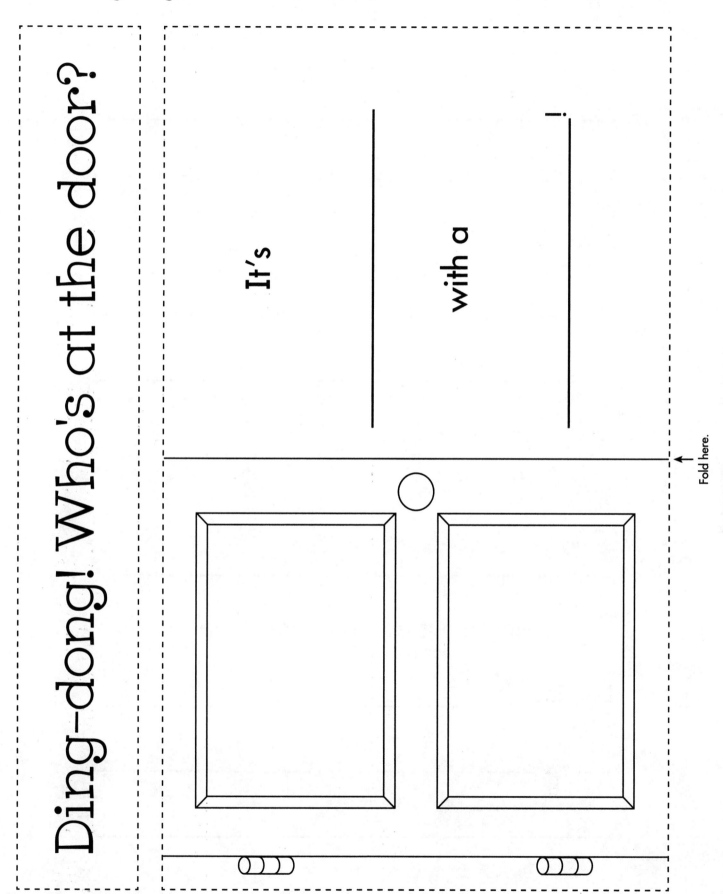

_____'s

enormous egg is extraordinary

because it _____

_____

_____.

_____'s

enormous egg is extraordinary

because it _____

_____

_____.

Funny Faces ✳ Text Boxes

Here are _____'s
funny faces. Find your favorite!

Here are _____'s
funny faces. Find your favorite!

Here are _____'s
funny faces. Find your favorite!

Guess what

is growing
in the garden!

Guess what

is growing
in the garden!

Guess what

is growing
in the garden!

Guess what

is growing
in the garden!

Ice Cream Inventions

Ice Cream Scoop

Ice Cream Inventions

Ice Cream Cone
and Text Box

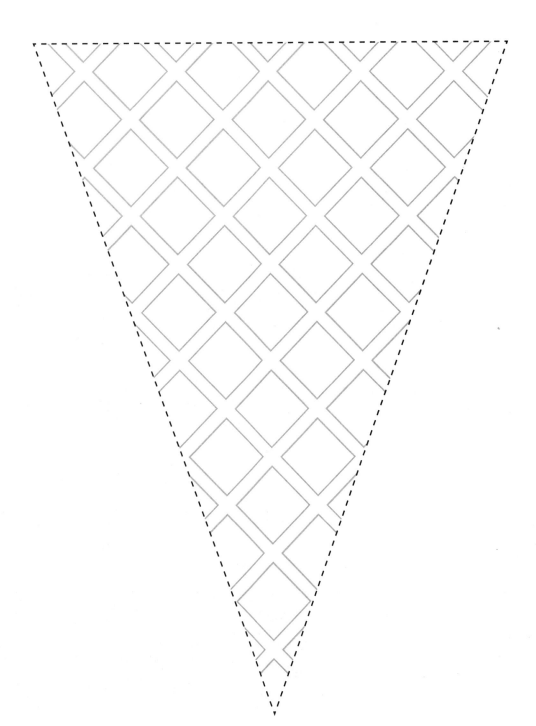

If I invented an ice cream flavor, it would be...

Jack and Jill Jump

Characters

❄ ❄ ❄

Keep Up Your Kite!

Text Box

❄ ❄ ❄

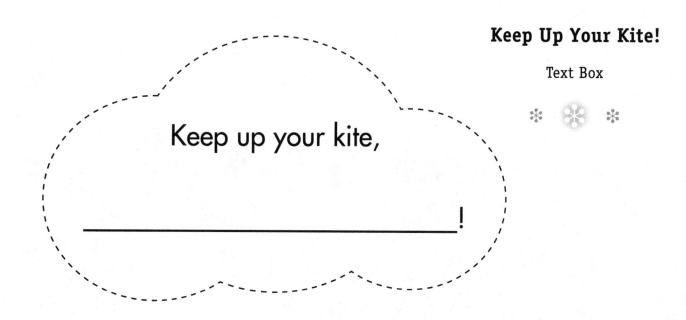

Keep up your kite,

_____!

Lovely Ladybugs

Ladybug Body

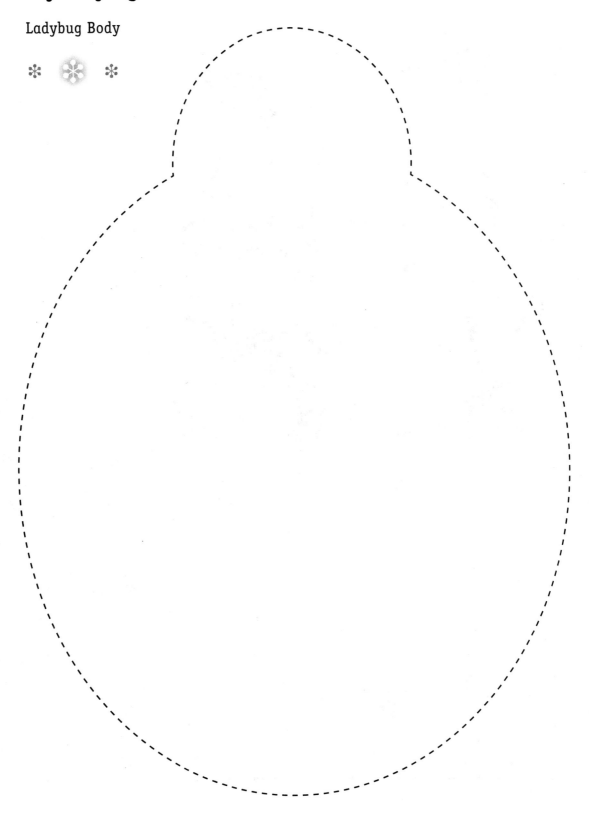

Lovely Ladybugs ✳ Text Box

_____'s lovely ladybug

has _____ little dots. Count them.

Near at Night ✳ Text Box

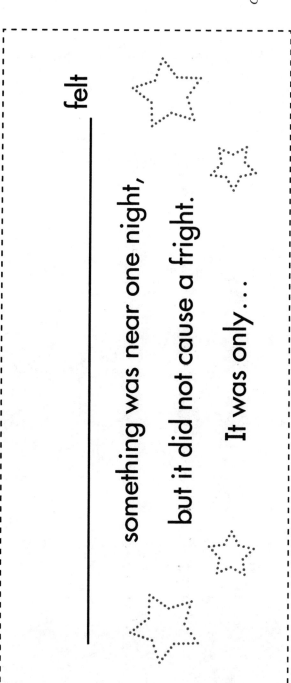

felt _____

something was near one night,

but it did not cause a fright.

It was only . . .

Collaborative Class Books From A to Z,
© 2014 by Ada Goren,
Scholastic Teaching Resources

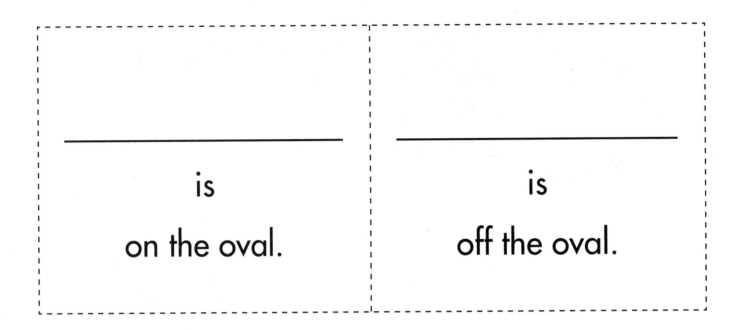

_____

is

on the oval.

_____

is

off the oval.

Put Some on My Plate, Please!

Text Box

❋ ❋ ❋

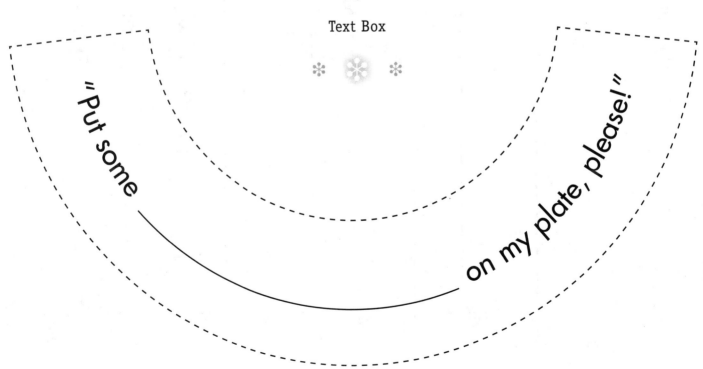

"Put some _____ on my plate, please!"

What Is Quiet? ❋ Text Boxes

A _____ is quiet.

A _____ is quiet.

Our Rectangle Robots ❋ Text Boxes

_____'s rectangle robot

is named _____.

_____'s rectangle robot

is named _____.

Silly Soup ✳ Bowl

____'s silly soup

is made with _____

and _____.

Collaborative Class Books From A to Z
© 2014 by Ada Goren, Scholastic Teaching Resources

Silly Soup ✳ Soup

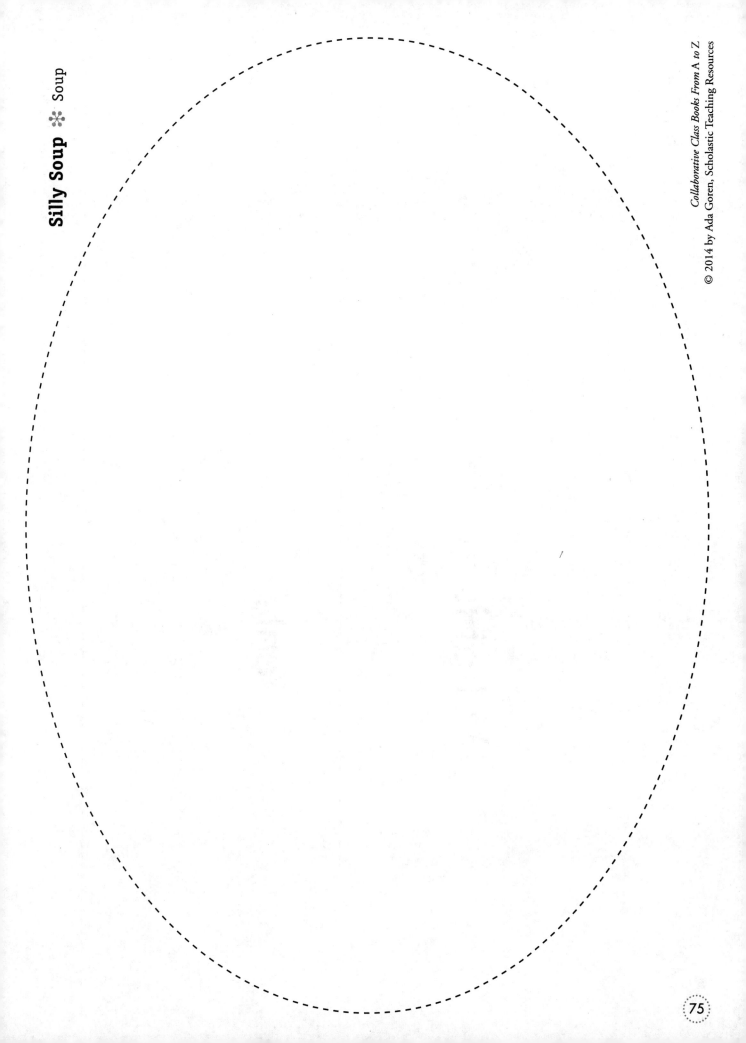

Tent

What is in

's

tent?

Collaborative Class Books From A to Z © 2013 by Ada Goren, Scholastic Teaching Resources

Uh-oh!
We're Upside-Down!

Text Box

A Very
Strange Vine

Leaf

Uh-oh!

_____ is upside-down!

One very sunny day,

_____'s class

saw a very strange vine.

Growing on the vine was . . .

Excellent X-rays ✳ Text Box

What an excellent x-ray of

_____ 's hand!

Yummy or Yucky? ✳ Text Boxes

Yum! :)

_____

likes

_____ !

Yuck! :(

_____

does not like

_____ !

Zero Zebras at the Zoo

Zoo Animals

Zero Zebras at the Zoo

Zoo Animals and Text Box

❄

❄

❄

_____'s zoo has

and zero zebras.